PRAIS
THE STREN

C000052764

"Everyone has strengths. This wonderfully insightful guide will help you discover yours – it could transform your work and life experiences."

DENISE WILSON OBE
Chief Executive, Hampton-Alexander Review

"The Strengths Book *is a 'must read' on your journey of personal development and long-term happiness."*

DAVID COX
CFO, UBM Americas

"This book gives a refreshingly simple, yet powerful new way to think about your life and what you're suited to career-wise. It could change your life."

NIGEL RUSSELL
Distribution Manager, BBC

"The queen of strengths has done it again, delivering a simple way for us all to identify our own strengths and apply that knowledge to our professional and personal lives. Thank you Sally – a must read for EVERYONE!"

JAMES DARLEY
Director of Strategic Alliances, Teach First

"This book is full of straightforward advice that people can use to make a real difference in their lives. Knowing what we love and are energized by is the key to a fulfilling career. Knowing their strengths early on could change a young person's life!"

IAN SHIPSEY

Associate Head, Department of Physics and Professorial Fellow, St. Catherine's College, University of Oxford

"This is more than a book, it's a practical guide for anyone interested in defining their brilliant self."

BERTIE TONKS

Global Director for People & Culture, Collinson

"This book challenges the idea that we have to be different to be better. In fact, excellence and fulfilment come from knowing our strengths and being more of ourselves. It's a no-nonsense approach with practical exercises to help you be the best you can be, no matter what your circumstances."

FARAN JOHNSON

HR Director, HM Courts and Tribunals Service

"Many societies, businesses and education systems define success in narrow ways and put enormous pressure on people to achieve it. This book gives an important and inspiring alternative point of view. It encourages people to value their strengths, whatever they may be, and it offers clear, practical advice on how to identify and play to them."

EMILY EVANS

Chief Executive, The Economist Educational Foundation

FOR OTHER TITLES IN THE SERIES...

CONCISE ADVICE LAB

SMALL BOOKS: BIG IDEAS

Published by
LID Publishing
An imprint of LID Business Media Ltd.
LABS House, 15-19 Bloomsbury Way,
London, WC1A 2TH, UK

info@lidpublishing.com
www.lidpublishing.com

A member of:

businesspublishersroundtable.com

© Sally Bibb, 2022
© LID Business Media Limited, 2022

Printed by Imak Ofset

ISBN: 978-1-911687-55-9
ISBN: 978-1-911687-60-3 (ebook)

Cover and page design: Caroline Li

THE STRENGTHS BOOK

**DISCOVER HOW TO BE FULFILLED
IN YOUR WORK AND IN LIFE**

SALLY BIBB

MADRID | MEXICO CITY | LONDON
BUENOS AIRES | BOGOTA | SHANGHAI

CONTENTS

INTRODUCTION   xi

THE STRENGTHS REVOLUTION   xvi

**PART ONE   WHAT ARE STRENGTHS AND WHY
              ARE THEY IMPORTANT?**   1
1. Why don't we talk about strengths?   3
2. Outdated ideas to let go of   5
3. What is a strength?   10
4. Why are strengths important?   12
5. How are strengths formed?   14
6. Knowing your strengths   16
7. Strengths drive our behaviour   18
8. What can you change about yourself?   20
9. What about weaknesses?   22
10. Can a weakness become a strength?   25
11. Why we focus on weaknesses – the negativity bias   26

PART TWO   IDENTIFYING YOUR STRENGTHS   35
1. What psychometric tests can't tell you   37
2. Your Strengths Profile   39
3. What do you love to do?   43
4. What makes you feel strong?   45
5. Identifying your strengths   48

6.	Confirming your strengths	53
7.	What do others think?	55
8.	Dislikes and weaknesses	57
9.	Overdone strengths	60

PART THREE	**DEVELOPING YOUR STRENGTHS**	65
1.	Why develop your strengths?	68
2.	How to develop your strengths	69
3.	How strengths work together	70
4.	How strengths mitigate weaknesses	72
5.	Skills and knowledge	73
6.	Using your strengths in different areas of life	74
7.	The Four A's strategy	76

PART FOUR	**APPLYING YOUR STRENGTHS**	81
1.	Planning to use your strengths in everyday life	84
2.	Using and developing your strengths at work	86
3.	Using your strengths to get a new job	90
4.	The strengths approach for leaders	95
5.	Using your strengths in your studies	99
6.	Using strengths in parenting	103
7.	Using strengths in relationships	107
8.	Using strengths in retirement	110

**PART FIVE WHAT ELSE DO YOU NEED TO
BE FULFILLED?**   117

1. What's important to you?   120
2. What motivates you?   125
3. What you can control and what you can't   128
4. Choosing your response   131
5. Your 'team'   134

CONCLUSION   137
EXAMPLE STRENGTHS PROFILE   139
MY STRENGTHS PROFILE   142
REFERENCES   146
FURTHER READING   148
ACKNOWLEDGEMENTS   149
ABOUT THE AUTHOR   150

INTRODUCTION

"Knowing your strengths changes your life. If you keep trying to be someone you're not you'll always be frustrated."

Why have we never been taught what it takes to be truly happy and satisfied with the big choices we make in life? Choices like which subjects to study at university, which career we would be well-suited to and how to get the best from ourselves and others?

If we knew these things early in life it could save a lot of unhappiness, frustration and, for some people, the feeling of having wasted years on the wrong things.

And even if you're one of those people who is lucky enough to have found a career that is right for you, do you know why it's right and do you know how to really make the most of it?

Whether you're happy with where you are in life now or not, do you know:

- What *exactly* makes you happy, so you can choose the things that will make you happy and avoid those that don't?
- How to decide whether a job, activity or course is right for you?
- Why things seem to just flow with some activities and not with others?

Knowing these things about yourself means you can spend more time on the things that energize and fulfill you. It means you can make the most of your one precious life. And it means that you can help those you care about do the same.

Read this book and discover what makes you tick – essential if you're to have a fulfilled life. Once you know your strengths, finding fulfilment is a lot easier than you might think. And a lot faster.

THIS BOOK AND HOW TO USE IT

Part One explains what strengths are, how they're formed and why they are so important to our happiness. It debunks some myths too. If you're the type of person who likes theory and rationale, that's also in there.

Part Two is where you get to discover your own strengths. You'll find plenty of exercises designed to appeal to different types of people.

Parts Three and Four are all about how to develop your strengths and apply them in different parts of your life.

Part Five takes you through other factors that are important for your fulfilment.

You will be able to start implementing what you learn straight away. And the value of what you will discover will stay with you for the rest of your life. Not only that, but you will be able to help other people – your friends, family and colleagues.

MY JOURNEY

This book matters a lot to me because, had I known about strengths when I was younger, I would have pushed harder to study for the degree that I really wanted to do, I would have refused promotion into a job that I wasn't cut out for and, in doing so, I would have saved myself a lot of frustration and unhappiness.

Let me take you back to the 1980s. I was in my 20s and a graduate doing a fabulous job in an exciting global organization. I was responsible for crewing cable ships that went around the world installing and repairing submarine telecommunications cables. I loved it. I was a round peg in a round hole and I couldn't wait to get to work every morning.

But then, it all went horribly wrong.

I was promoted. At first I was pleased – a move up the ladder, more pay, higher status and all the things that make us believe that promotion is progression.

The new job couldn't have been a worse fit for me. It involved doing desk research in preparation for my bosses' negotiations with the Trade Unions. I sat in a quiet office with my manager. They sent me on a data analysis course and, although I became competent enough with figures and spreadsheets, I found the work draining. In contrast, my previous job totally energized me.

My confidence dropped and neither my boss nor I could really understand how it was that I was so vibrant and successful in my previous role but not in my new one. I had ticked all the boxes in the interview but it didn't occur to any of us to ask whether it was actually a good fit for me.

Needless to say, I didn't last long in that job. But this played on my mind – how could an organization with such apparently sophisticated selection approaches have got it so wrong? It couldn't have been them; it must have been me. Or so I thought.

It took me ten years to work out what had happened.

It was while at a conference that I learned about the psychology of strengths, and how it could revolutionize people's lives. Then the light bulb moment – I was not playing to my strengths. In fact, I was spending most of my time trying to work around my weaknesses.

I was a square peg in a round hole.

My company was inadvertently trying to make me into something that I am not.

Now, almost 30 years later, thousands of people are still struggling in jobs to which they're not suited, and organizations are still getting it wrong.

Had I known about the importance of strengths and discovered my own earlier, I would have saved myself a lot of angst and made some better decisions.

I'm writing this book because I want to spread the word about the transformative power of knowing and using your strengths.

YOUR JOURNEY
This book is for you if you:

- Think there may be something out there that is better suited to you.
- Want to be really sure you are choosing a course of study or a career path in which you will be happy and thrive.
- Are discontented in your current job or career and want to find something you truly love doing.

Or simply...

- Are interested in discovering a path to becoming more energized and effective in life, work and relationships.

THE STRENGTHS REVOLUTION

Knowing about strengths is changing people's lives radically. Thousands of people are discovering work they love, embarking on previously overlooked paths because they've discovered their strengths.

"I feel happy and fulfilled now and completely at peace with who I am and what I do — not something I ever felt before in my life."

Having worked in the field of strengths for nearly a decade, I've come to realize that the approach appeals to, and helps, people of all ages and walks of life. Through my business, Engaging Minds, my colleagues and I have worked with students, nurses, coffee shop baristas, care assistants, shop workers, call centre agents, team leaders, senior executives, scientists, prison officers, HR professionals, receptionists, delivery drivers, customer service representatives, sales people, teachers... the list goes on. Regardless of who they are or the job they do, people love discovering their strengths. They find it energizing and liberating.

We've worked with people in 20 different countries, in a variety of sectors, including engineering, financial services, healthcare, justice, manufacturing, restaurants, retail, science and travel.

We've encountered very different people in very different contexts, but with one thing in common – they all have strengths. And, with few exceptions, they had no idea what their strengths were or how to make the most of them.

This is not the preserve of the privileged middle classes, as a City trader once suggested to me. No. This is the work of understanding and helping any human being – anywhere in the world and at any stage of their life – to discover who they really are and find rewarding paths.

FOR INDIVIDUALS, COACHES, LEADERS TEACHERS AND PARENTS

This book is for anyone who is interested in creating a more fulfilling and productive personal life or work life. It's also for those who want to help them.

- It's a tool for coaches to give to their coaching clients.
- It's for teachers to give to their students.
- It's a tool for leaders and managers to help them develop their people.
- It's for careers officers to help young people make decisions about their future.
- It's for parents who want to help their children find fulfilment.

PART ONE

WHAT ARE STRENGTHS AND WHY ARE THEY IMPORTANT?

THIS PART ANSWERS THE FOLLOWING QUESTIONS:

- What are strengths and why are they important?
- Why are strengths key to being happy and good at what you do?
- Why do weaknesses usually not matter?

"Focusing on your strengths gives you confidence. You can see the physical changes in people. It's amazing."

KEY FACTS:

- We spend about a third of our lives working.
- Only 13% of workers worldwide are happy at work[1].
- More than half of the UK's workers say they are in the wrong career[2].

"Few people, even highly successful people, can answer the questions: Do you know what you're good at? Do you know what you need to learn so that you get the full benefit of your strengths? Few have even asked themselves these questions."

– Peter F. Drucker

Before we get started with looking at the importance of strengths and (in Part Two) discovering YOUR strengths, there are a few ideas and practices that we need to debunk.

1. WHY DON'T WE TALK ABOUT STRENGTHS?

There are a few 'objections' people sometimes raise to using their strengths and telling others about them. I want to address these before we go any further.

- **It's bragging or showing off.** You can understand why people might think that way, especially if they live in a culture, or have been brought up in a family, where being modest is prized. It can come across as bragging if you start telling people how good you are at something. Instead, think about how, in addition to helping you, your strengths can be helpful to others. But, if people don't know what contribution you have to make, they will not ask for your help. It all depends how you say it. For example, if you were to say, "Oh I'd love to be on that team because I am great at x," this comment comes across very differently than, "I'd love to help and I've got a particular strength in x, so I think I could make a real contribution."

- **It's self-centred.** Sometimes people feel that to want to work on projects or parts of projects that play to their strengths is self-centred. However, it helps everyone if each member of a team can capitalize on what they are good at. And, it's actually the opposite of self-centred because it means that you can compensate for what your colleagues are weak at and vice versa.

- **It's irresponsible.** I've heard the strengths approach criticized for being irresponsible, in that it encourages people to focus on their own strengths and ignore their weaknesses. In fact, it's exactly the opposite because the responsible thing is to let others know where you can make the greatest contribution. And it's not about ignoring your weaknesses; it's about making clear where you can make the strongest impact. And it's about knowing realistically what you can do about your weaknesses.

I love what Marcus Buckingham said in his book, *Go Put Your Strengths to Work*[3]:

"The team doesn't need from you some vague willingness to 'do whatever it takes'. It needs you to understand your strengths and weaknesses in vivid detail and then take it upon yourself to figure out how to navigate towards the strengths and away from the weaknesses."

2. OUTDATED IDEAS TO LET GO OF

- **You should aim to be a well-rounded person.** Much of our school and work life seems designed around making us 'well-rounded' people. We are expected to achieve good grades in all our subjects and a good standard of performance in our company. This is unrealistic and undesirable.

  Imagine if British tennis pro Andy Murray had tried to be outstanding at everything. He probably would have been unhappier and much less proficient in sport because a large proportion of his energy would have been used up on things he didn't really like and was never going to be good at. None of us can be good at everything. If we spend time and energy trying to be good at everything we will become mediocre at many things and not great at anything.

- **You don't have enough strengths and need to develop more.** As you read this book, you will discover that you have a set of strengths and, if you put these to work, they will make you happy and great at what you do. The idea that people are lacking strengths is incorrect. We all have strengths – the problem is most people either don't know what their strengths are, take them for granted, or are unsure how to use them to their best advantage.

- **Excellent performance comes from fixing our weaknesses.** The assumption in organizations is that to achieve excellence, weaknesses have to be eradicated as much as possible. Many, if not most, employers take people's strengths for granted and focus on getting them to fix their weaknesses. This leads to mediocre performance at best. It certainly doesn't result in motivated, confident employees.

  It also means that most of an organization's training budget is spent on trying to fix weaknesses rather than developing people to be even better in their areas of strength. Ideally, an organization's resources should be spent selecting the right people for roles in which they will be a great fit in the first place.

- **You need to be different to be better.** For most of us, the exact opposite is true. You actually need to be more of who you *really* are, deep down, to be better. Sure, you might need to gain new awareness, knowledge or skills to add to the raw materials of 'you' but if you keep trying to be different you will always be frustrated.

  In order to be excellent people don't have to change. They just have to understand who they are and what their innate strengths are. Then they need to work on those things like crazy until they become excellent.

- **It's unrealistic to expect to enjoy your job.** The idea that we should just get on and put up with work we don't enjoy is deep-rooted. It possibly has its origins in an era where a lot of people worked in awful jobs and harsh conditions; when work was simply a matter of survival and not an opportunity for self-expression. Nowadays, it's reasonable to expect to get much more out of working than our pay. If you know what makes you tick, you can find fulfilment in work.

- **Progressing means climbing the career ladder.** It's been an unchallenged assumption for years that getting on means moving upwards in the organization's hierarchy. Do you know anyone who was promoted from a job they were happy in to a managerial role only to realize they didn't like managing and weren't very good at it? It's apparently quite common.

  Since Generation Y (otherwise known as the 'Millennials') entered the workforce, however, that notion has been challenged. Generation Y are less inclined to think of progression as vertical, but rather as horizontal growth. This is more about the notion of 'fit'. The question should always be, are you a good fit?

  This different way of thinking can be hard for people to get used to because it's not a common practice. But it is common sense. I had a conversation with a nurse who, while she hadn't thought about it too much, had always assumed that her next career move would be a rung up the ladder to the position of Ward Sister. What she actually discovered was that she loved being a nurse. She loved the day-to-day contact with patients and she actually didn't love being in charge. During our discussion she realized that she would be a round peg in a square hole as a Ward Sister. Far from being disappointed she was actually relieved to have realized this when she did.

- **Having a career is superior to having a job.** The idea of a career being superior to a job is probably to do with notions of personal fulfilment, satisfaction, contribution to society and achievement of potential. There is certainly more status attached to having a career than there is to having a job. A job is often thought of as something someone simply does for the money rather than gaining any intrinsic satisfaction from it.

This thinking is challenged by the strengths movement, which, instead of focusing on jobs versus careers, encourages exploring the route to satisfaction. Working in a call centre could be considered 'just a job'. So could working in a coffee shop or as a delivery driver. But, actually, what we have discovered in our work with many people in all sorts of organizations is that there are those in all of the aforementioned roles who actually love their job and say things like, "I can't believe I get paid to do this." The point is, everyone has strengths, so it makes no difference whether you call your work a job or career. What matters is that you get to love what you do every day.

- **Positive thinking leads to happiness.** The positive thinking movement encourages people to be positive even when they're not feeling positive. It asserts that to be happy you simply need to think positively. The research shows that if we try and push emotions like sadness, grief and anger to one side we actually become less happy[4].

Happiness is a by-product of doing things that we find intrinsically valuable. It's not a state you can achieve by just changing your thoughts. So, if you're unhappy at work, at college or in your relationship, thinking positively won't change that. In fact, it may even make it worse because you will feel that you should be able to shift into a positive frame of mind and, if you can't, you may believe there is something wrong with you.

"I'm so much happier working with what I've got rather than wasting time and energy trying to be something I'm not."

EXERCISE

Have a look at the examples below and write your own beliefs and their replacements in the spaces provided:

What beliefs do I have that are untrue or don't help me	What can I replace this with
I'm not successful if I don't get promoted	*I will be truly successful if I am in a job that I love and am a natural fit for*
I'm somehow lacking	*I have all the strengths I need, I just need help to identify, value and apply them*

3. WHAT IS A STRENGTH?

A strength is something that someone is naturally good at, loves doing and is energized by.

Our strengths are innate. They are developed by the time we reach our mid-teens. By then we are who we are and we don't change very much after that. We can learn new skills or acquire new knowledge but what we are like as a person fundamentally doesn't change all that much.

An example of an innate strength is loving to connect with other people. Have you ever noticed how great baristas in coffee shops do this? They can't help it – they can't *not* do it. Another example is the athlete who is naturally competitive. They just have to win. It's part of who they are.

Think of your strengths as something that you can't *not* do. They are the things that feel like a natural part of who you are. Take a moment to think about what that means to you. What sort of things do you naturally do? Is it that you almost always:

- Talk to people in lifts, queues or on trains?
- Have a list of things to do, even at weekends?
- Strive to always finish first?
- See problems that need solving?

If you said a big "Yes, that's me!" to any of these things it's an indication that it's one of your strengths.

Using our strengths energizes us. If you answered "No" to any of these, chances are it's because it's not one of your natural strengths. These are the things you would probably avoid doing, and if you did them they would drain you.

Our values are also strengths. For example, it may be very important to you to make a difference.

Our motivators are strengths too. You may be motivated by being competitive, or by being extremely organized.

Your strengths reflect the real you. You can't NOT be this way.

4. WHY ARE STRENGTHS IMPORTANT?

Have you ever felt like you were trying to be something you're not? Or that you were doing a job where you were expected to be something you're not?

Chances are that you were feeling this way because you were doing things that you were not cut out to do. This was what happened to me when I was promoted into a job that involved hours working on spreadsheets. I learned the knowledge and skills to be good enough at it, but I lacked the excitement for numbers and data so I was never going to love it.

Our strengths are important because:

- They are the real us. What's the point in going against the grain of who we are when we can thrive by being more of who we actually are?
- They make us confident because they are us at our best – they're the things we're naturally good at.
- We can let go of the idea that we should be different in some way.

And the big thing about strengths is they mean we get to live *our* life, not somebody else's!

Our strengths are important because living a life where we spend most of our time playing to our strengths is the only way to be satisfied.

If you don't know your strengths you could spend your life being miserable because you will always try to be something you're not.

Understanding your strengths can change your life because when you realize what you're naturally good at you will experience an enormous boost in confidence and sense of excitement about yourself. It also leads to self-acceptance because it makes clear what is positive about you, much of which you may have been taking for granted before or simply didn't realize.

I know it changes people's lives because I've seen people of all ages become very emotional when they find out about their strengths. Not just because they are gaining very affirming and positive insight into themselves, but also because they realize how fundamentally this can change their life and the lives of those around them.

We live in a time when the pressure to succeed is great. Education systems around the world are very driven by results. Young people feel pressure to perform. And businesses push their employees to meet myriad targets and perform ever better. There is nothing wrong with that per se. It becomes a problem when a person feels under pressure to be something they are not. When they feel they have to achieve higher in all subjects and they can't accept that they aren't excellent at everything.

Too many parents, teachers and organizations are inadvertently trying to make us into something we're not.

"I'm in a role I'm naturally suited for. People say things to me like, 'You were born to do this'."

5. HOW ARE STRENGTHS FORMED?

Our strengths are created by synapses in the brain. A synapse is a connection between two brain cells that enables the neurons to communicate. These synapses are your threads – and behaviour depends on the formation of appropriate electrical and chemical interconnections among neurons in the brain. Simply put, your synapses create your strengths.

On day 42 after conception, the brain creates its first neuron. Some 120 days later the brain will have 100 billion. That is 9,500 neurons every second. Roughly 60 days before birth, neurons start to communicate with each other and make connections. By the age of three, each of the 100 billion neurons have formed 15,000 synaptic connections with other neurons. But then things take a strange turn. Nature prompts a lot of the woven threads to be ignored, and as these get neglected they fall into disuse and connections start to break. Between the ages of 3 and 15 the brain will lose billions of these synaptic connections. By age 16 ½ the network is essentially gone, and it can't be rebuilt. Genetic inheritance and early childhood experiences help make finding some connections smoother and easier to use than others. Through lack of use some of these dwindle, while others are nurtured, used and honed so that they become very well established. By the time we reach puberty these synaptic connections are set and not a lot of change happens after that.

Think of it this way: our strengths are like a four-lane superhighway of the brain. The connections that are fast and efficient are those that are used often and are well trodden. The connections that are used less often are like a minor road that's unfamiliar, more difficult to navigate and not an enjoyable experience.

Our strengths are formed by puberty. By then we are who we are and don't change that much.

6. KNOWING YOUR STRENGTHS

When people become really clear about what their strengths are they often become more motivated and settled just because of that knowledge. Knowing our strengths allows us to understand more clearly why we are happy in certain situations and not in others. And that allows us to deliberately seek out those situations. Here are some examples:

Caroline is a fund-raiser. Her strengths include loving to meet new people, relating to others, curiosity, determination and making a difference. She told me that discovering her strengths meant she stopped questioning herself about whether she is in the right job. Now she knows she is because she uses her strengths all the time. Elizabeth is a recent graduate. She wasn't a very confident person until she realized that, despite having little work experience, she has a lot of strengths. She loves achieving, she likes to help others, she is excellent at communicating and she's very motivated by learning new things. These are all things she hadn't thought about before and hadn't put in her CV. Knowing she has all these attributes has given her confidence that she has something to offer potential employers.

Ed is a trainee journalist. He has autism. He was struggling to get interviews. Some of his strengths are listening, doing the right thing, communicating clearly in writing, determination and organization – all strengths that are valuable to a journalist. He added a Strengths Profile into his CV, started getting interviews and feels really confident talking about himself at interviews now because he feels he can express his real self.

7. STRENGTHS DRIVE OUR BEHAVIOUR

Think of your strengths as the deep bit of you. They are the engine that drives how you act. For example, if you're a person who loves to take responsibility, that behaviour will show itself when you offer to take on projects, or make that tough customer phone call that needs to be made but nobody else seems willing to handle.

Our strengths can also mean that we sometimes behave in a way that is uncomfortable or unnatural. For example, if you're not an assertive person by nature, but doing the right thing is really important to you, you may have noticed yourself being assertive to make sure things are done right – even though you might have been shaking inside. I witnessed this very thing one day when I saw a nurse standing up to a doctor. She wasn't a naturally assertive person but because the doctor was compromising her patient's wellbeing by his actions she told him so, though she felt intimidated and it was nerve-wracking for her to do so. She wouldn't be the sort of person who would send a lukewarm meal back in a restaurant but that is because the lukewarm meal wouldn't matter that much to her. But, in the scenario with the doctor, one of her key strengths – a compulsion to do the right thing – prompted a behaviour that is not natural to her.

Our behaviour is just a by-product of our strengths. This means that we can use our strengths to behave in ways that might not be easy for us but that will help us achieve our goal.

8. WHAT CAN YOU CHANGE ABOUT YOURSELF?

Our strengths don't change because they are an intrinsic part of who we are. We may start using strengths that we previously haven't used all that much, and they might develop and get stronger with use. Or they may weaken and fade if we don't use them. But they are always there.

We can change our behaviour but what thrills us or drains us stays fairly constant over time.

Ok, so we've established that we can't – and shouldn't try to – change who we fundamentally are (i.e., our strengths). So, what can we change?

- We can learn new skills.
- We can acquire new knowledge.
- We can (to some extent) change our behaviour.

For instance, you may find that you have a key ingredient for succeeding as a manager – you love to be in charge. But you have no idea how to give feedback or run a team meeting. It is important to realize that these are skills you can learn. You may need to know something about employment law, for example. This is knowledge you can acquire by reading or taking courses.

You can't change what you are fundamentally like as a person. But you can learn new skills and acquire new knowledge.

9. WHAT ABOUT WEAKNESSES?

Some employers use the euphemism 'areas for development' instead of 'weaknesses', because the word weaknesses has negative connotations. I can see why they do this, but it seems crazy because weaknesses are not negative at all. Every one of us has weaknesses, just as every one of us has strengths. It's part of being human.

So, first and foremost, don't be ashamed of weaknesses. We need to accept that we have them and then decide whether we need to do something about them or not.

But, before we get on to that, it's helpful to split weaknesses into two types: those that matter and those that don't. Most of our weaknesses are irrelevant because they don't get in the way of our performance. For example, if you are a journalist and you are not very good at fixing things around the house, it doesn't matter. But a newspaper journalist who isn't good at communicating clearly using the written word will never be a very good journalist.

List your main weaknesses in the table on page 24. Then categorize them into the ones that don't matter, those that sometimes matter and the ones that get in the way of you performing excellently.

Here's an example, created by someone who organizes conferences:

Weakness	Doesn't matter (I can ignore them)	Sometimes matters	Matters	Ways of mitigating those that matter
Not very good at leading	X			
Terrible at handling conflict		X		Next time a conflict arises, think about what matters about resolving it as that can help give me the courage to face it. Also ask a colleague who is comfortable with conflict to help when needed (e.g., help draft assertive emails).
Not good at analyzing data	X			
Struggles to be assertive			X	This is linked to not liking conflict so the same 'workarounds' apply. Could also take an assertiveness course to learn some tips and techniques.

List your own weaknesses here.

Weakness	Doesn't matter (I can ignore it)	Sometimes matters	Matters	Ways of mitigating those that matter

Instead of feeling constrained by your weaknesses, switch your thinking to see them as part of what it means to be human. Focus only on the weaknesses that matter - those that are relevant to achieving your goals - and on doing the things that are important to you.

10. CAN A WEAKNESS BECOME A STRENGTH?

If something is genuinely a weakness, we cannot turn it into a strength. You may be able to improve it or use one of your strengths to allow you to enjoy it more. For example if you don't like being in the spotlight and so dislike public speaking, you might become more comfortable with it with practice. You may also learn some skills and techniques to get better at it. You may, as one of my clients did, realize that it's a way to achieve something that's really important to you such as getting a message out to the world that you care about.

The likelihood is, if you think you have a strength now that used to be a weakness, one of the following explanations applies; you didn't realize it was actually a strength; you've developed the confidence to use it and see it as a strength; or something else in your environment has changed which means you feel you have the freedom to apply that strength.

11. WHY WE FOCUS ON WEAKNESSES - THE NEGATIVITY BIAS

We know from evolutionary biology and neuroscience that we are programmed to be alert to risks in our environment. Therefore, it's human nature to focus more on the negative. Early humans had to worry about wild animals and neighbouring tribes so it was essential to focus on potential problems. People who were alert to risk in their environment were more likely to survive.

In today's context that translates to focusing on what is not working, including ignoring the good pieces of feedback that we're given, and obsessing about the one negative thing someone says. This one negative thing can totally overshadow all the positives, resulting in disproportionate energy being used up on the area that is not the greatest driver of excellence.

Just becoming aware of the negativity bias can protect us against its most damaging effects. If we start to notice it in ourselves and others we can work on balancing it with a focus on the positive.

If a person has a really strong negativity bias it can affect others as well as themselves. Think about your work or family environment. When some people walk into a room your heart lifts and you think, "Oh good, it's so-and-so." When other people walk in, your heart sinks a bit and you're probably polite but you're not genuinely keen to engage with them. That can be because the first types are the yea-sayers – those who are generally positive and good to be around. The second types are the naysayers, who can be dispiriting and draining.

So understanding this negativity bias and its impact on yourself and others is really important because of the energy and time it can drain away from you. It can be an insidious thing that prevents you from being the best possible you.

As we've said, focusing on what's wrong instead of what's right is human nature – it's a basic survival instinct. However, in the modern world it can be damaging to motivation, morale and performance.

EXERCISE
RE-SETTING A NEGATIVE DEFAULT MODE AND BOOSTING YOUR CONFIDENCE

If, like many people, you tend to focus on what you're not very good at more than what you're really good at, have a go at this exercise:

1. Ask three people who know you very well, and whom you respect, to email or message you a list of things they think you're really good at. Writing it down helps them take the time to think about it and receiving it in writing adds weight.

_____

_____

2. Log these in a place where you can easily see them, like your phone or notebook.

_____

_____

3. Whenever you find yourself thinking about what you're not very good at, read this list.

_____

_____

_____

EXERCISE
BOOSTING YOUR CONFIDENCE

If you like physical activities and maybe fancy yourself as a bit of an actor, do this when you have a few minutes alone:

Stand up with the list you created on page 28 in your hand. Stand straight, with your arms in the air and your head looking upward. Take a few deep breaths and hold this pose for a few seconds. Then, as if you were on stage and projecting your voice, say, "I'm [your name], and some of my strengths are x, y, z." Put a lot of energy in your voice when you do this. Repeat several times, each time increasing the energy with which you speak. This may seem silly but there is evidence that this 'power pose' exercise influences your mood and confidence.

Amy Cuddy, professor and researcher at Harvard Business School, discovered how changing your physical pose affects your body chemistry and has a positive influence on how you perform and how others perceive you[5]. Anytime you feel lacking in confidence, about anything in your life, do this exercise. If you are in a place where you can't do it without feeling silly (such as on a bus on your way to an interview), imagine doing it. Run through it mentally. Even imagining it will have a positive effect on you.

EXERCISE
SHIFTING THE BALANCE FROM NEGATIVE TO POSITIVE

I'm not talking about becoming an annoying Pollyanna type, who portrays everything as positive when it clearly is not. I'm talking about shifting a focus to the positive when that is more likely to give you the outcome you want.

Try not to complain, criticize or gossip for 24 hours. When you catch yourself (we all probably do these things more than we think) mentally restart the exercise.

_____

_____

_____

_____

_____

_____

_____

_____

EXERCISE
THE POSITIVE ENERGY-GIVERS

Write a list of all the people in your life who tend to make you feel positive. Think about what they do that results in that. Try and spend more time with them and learn from what they do. Make note of all the attributes that person has. Highlight the ones that you intend to do more of yourself.

Positive behaviour and attitudes	Person's name	Person's name	Person's name
Greets people with a smile			
Laughs a lot			
Says positive things about others			
Gives compliments			
Hardly ever gossips			
Talks about positive things more than negative things			
Hardly ever criticizes			
Tends not to be judgmental			
Is appreciative			

IN SUMMARY

We all acquire certain beliefs that may not be true – beliefs such as, "Success means climbing the corporate ladder" or "I should be good at all the subjects I study". These assumptions can hold us back from doing what is right for us and steer us away from where we will thrive. Replacing these outdated or simply untrue ideas with ones that reflect the current reality is likely to help you find fulfilment in work, relationships and life in general.

One of the beliefs many people hold is that to be better you need to focus on fixing your weaknesses. In fact to be better you need to clearly understand and use your strengths.

Our strengths are those things that we are innately good at, love doing and are energized by. They are created and fixed in our behaviour by the time we're in our mid-teens. In other words, by then, we are who we are, and we don't change much after that. We can learn new skills and knowledge but fundamentally we remain the same person throughout our lives. The things we're drawn to, the things we can't leave alone, the things we love – they remain constant. If anything, they become more insistent forces in us as we get older.

Our strengths are key to our success and fulfilment. It's a simple and common sense concept but it's not something we're taught. Yet it can be life changing.

KEY TAKEAWAYS:

- Our strengths are the route to excellence and fulfilment.
- We all have strengths – the problem is that most people either don't know their strengths, take them for granted or are unsure how to use them to their best advantage.
- Be more of who you truly are; you don't need to be different.

PART TWO

IDENTIFYING
YOUR
STRENGTHS

THIS SECTION WILL ANSWER THE FOLLOWING QUESTIONS:

- What are you naturally good at?
- What do you love doing?
- What is your Strengths Profile?

KEY FACTS:

People who use their strengths more are:

- More confident, have higher levels of vitality and are happier.
- More resilient and less stressed.
- Higher performers and more likely to achieve their goals.

"Knowing your strengths changes your life in ways that you can't even begin to possibly imagine. You're surrounded by this positive energy and that has an effect on everyone you come into contact with and every experience that you have. It improves all your relationships, and even the way that you think. There's nothing that it won't touch."

1. WHAT PSYCHOMETRIC TESTS CAN'T TELL YOU

You may have taken psychometric tests at school, college or work and be wondering what the difference is between doing the exercises in this book and taking psychometric tests. The big difference is that psychometric tests look at ability and aptitude, whereas strengths assessments look at desire and innate motivation.

Think of it this way: a psychometric test tells you about **skill**, and a strengths assessment tells you about **will**.

And, as we all know, it's no good just being able to do something. To be energized and good at it you *need to want to do it*.

So, what can the exercises in this book give you that online or 'tick box' strengths tests can't? There are two things.

The first is that these exercises will make you think deeply about yourself. When we are given the opportunity to really think about ourselves and come to our own realizations, that touches us more deeply than filling in a questionnaire with pre-written, generic descriptors. Don't get me wrong, these can be useful... but they can never be sufficiently personalized. And because it's quite a passive process, where you fill in the questionnaire and receive a report, it's easy to think, "Oh that's interesting", put it to one side and never look at it again. So, in the long run, it will really make no difference in the day-to-day reality of your life. However, when you go through a guided reflection process to think about your strengths, you are thinking about them in your own way and in your own language. You also think about the implications and applications so that the insight you gain touches you more deeply and stays with you for longer – usually for life!

The second way in which these psychometrics and strengths diagnostics differ is that when you get a list of personality labels, like those contained in some of the personality profiling tools, you get a summary of your dominant patterns of thought or preference. These are just predispositions indicating that you behave in a certain way. Your strengths, on the other hand, are specific things you do really well and that you love doing. These go beyond this broad labeling and are about what we do on a day-to-day basis. So, for example, a personality test might tell you that you're conscientious. What it can't tell you is whether you have a specific strength in organizing things to create order.

2. YOUR STRENGTHS PROFILE

Use this section to capture insights and develop your 'Strengths Profile' (you can find this on page 142) as you go along. You can use it by yourself or, if you're working with a coach or mentor, it's a useful tool to work through with them. The insight you gain from this section will help you thrive and be fulfilled in your work and life.

Investing a bit of your time in this section could save you months, years or a lifetime of being unhappy in your career or job! In order to get the most from this section:

- Work through the exercises in any order you like. Some people like to go through from start to finish; others prefer to flip back and forth. It doesn't matter.
- If you run out of energy or get bored, stop for a while and come back to it later.
- If you want a 'quick fix' to motivate you to get going (or if you have no time) start with the first exercise.
- Some of the exercises have options to either write things down, draw things, talk about things or do something physical. This is because different modes appeal to different people. Choose whichever appeals to you the most, or do them all!

Whatever your age or circumstances you will learn things about yourself in this section that will enhance your life and will always stay with you.

Enjoy...

QUICK FIX

If you want an instant win from this book, complete this five-minute exercise. Answer these three questions as honestly as you can:

1. What did I do last week that I really loved doing and energized me? List as many activities as you can remember, however short.

    For example:
    I had a great call with a new client about the website I'm building for him, and he loved some new ideas I'd shown him. I punched the air afterwards!

2. What is it about me that makes me love those things so much?

    For example:
    I like sharing my creative ideas and seeing my client excited about them.

    I like collaborating to spark new ideas.

    I like knowing what the next step will be because it feels like progress is being made.

I like feeling I'm doing a good job and that my creative work is appreciated.

3. List all the strengths you used in the above activities and highlight the three that give you the biggest buzz.

For example:
I'm good at explaining/sharing/teaching my ideas.

I energize people and projects, and my work picks up momentum and makes progress – unless there are complicating factors outside of my control!

People often feel motivated and excited after talking to me about a project. I inspire people.

I encourage ideas generation – I make 'two heads are better than one' happen! People often say I make them think of something new, or that they feel better/clearer/more on top of things after a call with me.

I understand quickly what people need/want to showcase online and generally find that I can make it happen.

I'm good at keeping projects on track because I'm organized and conscientious.

Or, if you're a more visual person, draw your responses in any way that make sense to you or make a collage with images that fit.

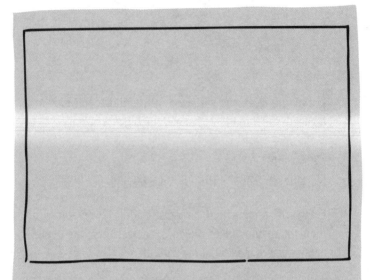

Alternatively, if you're more auditory, record yourself talking about this or speak to a friend or colleague about it.

If you're a very physical person, imagine three large squares on the ground, each representing one of the three questions. Stand in each square in sequence as you answer each question. Then, in the third square – representing the three strengths that give you the biggest buzz – strike a pose that embodies the spirit of the things that really give you a great buzz. Once you've done that make a few notes about what that was like for you.

YOUR PROFILE

Working through the following sections will help you to determine your own Strengths Profile. And if you'd like to see your profile in one neat format, flip to page 142 and complete the 'My Profile' template. You can then save, copy and refer to it whenever you'd like.

3. WHAT DO YOU LOVE TO DO?

One clue in discovering our strengths is to know that they are usually the things that we love to do.

Think of the things that give you a buzz, that you look forward to doing, that energize you, that you always check off your to-do list first.

If you're struggling to list many things, think about a recent situation you found really enjoyable or rewarding in some way. It might have made you feel happy or pleased with yourself. For example, you may have enjoyed meeting new people at a party, or spent time visiting someone in hospital, or being alone working on a particularly engaging project.

It could be anything, no matter how small it might seem. If you loved doing it, write about it. Here are a couple of examples to help you:

Things I enjoyed doing	What made me enjoy doing this?	What was it like?
Sitting with an elderly neighbour to give his wife a break	*I love helping people out and I like to care for people*	*I was happy to help; it felt worthwhile and made me feel good about myself*
Won someone over to support my project	*I love to achieve things and I'm also competitive so I like to be able to 'win'*	*I got a real buzz and felt on a high for ages*

If you're a more visual person, draw this in a way that appeals to you or make a collage with images that fit.

Or, if you're a physical or auditory person, draw three (real or imaginary) circles – one inside the other, on the ground. The outer one signifies the things you enjoyed; stand in it and think about those things. You can say them out loud too. Then step into the second circle and ask yourself what made you enjoy this. Then go into the innermost circle and ask yourself what that was like. Strike a pose that expresses what that was like for you or how it made you feel.

4. WHAT MAKES YOU FEEL STRONG?

Let's get into this section with a quick-fire idea. Our strengths are those things that, when we're doing them, make us feel strong. In contrast, something that makes you feel weak is a good definition of a weakness.

Without thinking about this too much, quickly write down as many activities as possible that make you feel strong and energized:

MY BEST SELF

Think about times when you were at your best. Include recollections from your personal life as well as experiences at work, studying, playing sports or engaging in hobbies. Anything at all. To help get the juices flowing, think of instances when you:

- Felt entirely present and alive.
- Were really true to yourself.
- Got a sense that you were fulfilling your potential.
- Experienced a deep sense of satisfaction.
- Had a vivid, memorable high.

Make a few notes or create some visuals about these situations.

Now answer these questions about the times that came to mind

- What exactly were you doing?

  _____

  _____

  _____

  _____

- What was that like?

  _____

  _____

  _____

  _____

- Do any common themes emerge?

  _____

  _____

  _____

  _____

5. IDENTIFYING YOUR STRENGTHS

Take a look at the strengths listed in the table below and ask yourself whether each one is very much like you, a bit like you or not very much like you. Put a check mark in the relevant box for each strength. When answering, think of yourself overall, in various settings and circumstances (at home, at work, at school or university and in your spare time).

Strength	Very much like me	A bit like me	Not very much like me
I love to be in charge: I am naturally drawn to take the lead in any situation			
I am a very competitive person: It's very important for me to be the best			
I have a lot of drive: I am never satisfied until I have achieved what I set out to do			
It's very important to me to do the right thing: I am the type of person who speaks up, or takes risks, if something is not right			

Strength	Very much like me	A bit like me	Not very much like me
I am honest and straightforward: People know where they stand with me			
I am naturally optimistic: I usually assume that things will turn out well			
I get a buzz out of learning: I continuously look for opportunities to develop and grow			
I love developing others: I get great satisfaction from watching others progress and realize their potential			
I instinctively tune in to other people's needs: I quickly realize if something is wrong with someone and am good at understanding situations from other peoples' perspectives			
I care about people: Others' wellbeing is really important to me			
I love making connections: I enjoy bringing people together for their mutual benefit			
I like making decisions: I thrive on weighing the options and selecting the best way forward			
I am good at analysing data and situations: I enjoy the challenge of making sense of complex and sometimes incomplete information			
I am always coming up with new ways of doing things: Creative thinking comes naturally to me			

Strength	Very much like me	A bit like me	Not very much like me
I thrive on solving problems: I enjoy the challenge of finding solutions to issues and challenges			
I have very high standards: I strive to achieve excellence			
I love to work with my hands: I get great satisfaction from doing practical tasks			
I am energized by working with other people: I love collaborating and being part of a team			
I am disciplined: I love to organize things so I achieve my deadlines			
I'm a very positive person: I tend to see the upside of things and people			

Which of the strengths did you mark as 'very much like me'? Of those, which do you think are the MOST like you? Write them down on the next page, and if any other strengths come to mind that are not on the list add those too. Also look at what you wrote for the previous exercises as this is information about your strengths as well.

My top strengths:

The more time you spend playing to your strengths, the happier you will be.

Ask yourself these questions and note your responses down:

- Roughly what proportion of time do I spend using my strengths?

_____

_____

_____

_____

- What kinds of people and situations really bring out my strengths?

_____

_____

_____

_____

- Could I make any changes, however small, that will result in me spending more time using my strengths?

_____

_____

_____

_____

6. CONFIRMING YOUR STRENGTHS

If you are unsure at this point whether you have identified your true strengths, use this test to check. Ask yourself the following questions in relation to each of your strengths.

Enthusiasm
- Do you mostly look forward to doing or being [insert name of strength]?
- Do you get a buzz out it?
- Is it something that you don't tend to put off doing?
- Does it feel like not much of an effort?
- Would you voluntarily use this strength/do this activity more if you could?

Success
- Do you think you're good at it?
- Have other people commented that you're good at it?
- Have you been given praise or recognition for this strength, or what you've achieved as a result of using it?

Ease

- Do you find that it comes fairly easily to you?
- Have you wondered why others find it much harder to do than you do?
- Have you always been this way?
- Does it feel natural to you?

If you've answered yes to most of these questions, the likelihood is that the strength in question is indeed one of your inherent, natural strengths. There is no 'correct score'. Your answers should reflect your instinctual, gut sense that this is part of the real you.

7. WHAT DO OTHERS THINK?

It's always interesting to hear how other people see you and what they think your strengths are. We can sometimes discover things we didn't realize about ourselves by asking others.

It's not often we get asked by friends or colleagues what they think we are good at. It can sound like we're fishing for compliments, and that can make us feel uncomfortable. Don't let this put you off because most people like to be asked to help, especially if you explain what a difference their help could make.

Tell a few people who know you well that you're doing this exercise, show them your top strengths and ask them if they agree that these are things you're naturally good at. Ask whether they can think of other natural strengths that you may have overlooked.

To take this deeper, choose a few people who you think would be happy to spend a bit of time on this – it could be work colleagues, a partner, family members, friends. Ask them to put their thoughts in writing, which will give them a chance to think about it and not just give their immediate, 'top of mind' response.

Once you've finished the exercise, and have written up your profile on page 142, read feedback from others and add any new insight.

Here are the sorts of question you could ask others about your personal strengths:

- One of the ways I add value and make an important contribution (to work, family, circle of friends) is _____

  _____

  _____.

- Do you recall a situation that illustrates this?

  _____

  _____

- What do you think I'm naturally good at?

  _____

  _____

- What have you observed gives me a buzz?

  _____

  _____

Now go to page 142 and complete your Strengths Profile using the insight you've gained about yourself so far. To help you, there is an example *(from Joe Bloggs on page 139)*.

8. DISLIKES AND WEAKNESSES

It might seem strange to be asked to think about things you don't much like doing in a book about strengths. Yet, it's important to think about this because it helps you get clearer about the contrast between what is and what isn't a great fit for you.

Think about the things you really don't like doing. What are the things that drain you, that always seem to stay at the bottom of your to-do list, that make your heart sink just thinking about them?

For some people, it could be organizing things, working through spreadsheets, or meeting new people. Others hate writing, having to achieve targets or following rules. It's fine not to like everything. We're all different. So, don't think about how you think you *should* be, and don't worry about what anyone would think if they read this. Just write it all down on the next page.

List things you dislike doing; include as many as you can think of.

The things we don't like doing are often also our weaknesses.

ALL of us have weaknesses. We wouldn't be human if we didn't. Some of our weaknesses might have an impact on the job we're doing or on what we're studying, while others won't.

Think through your areas of weakness.

List your weaknesses below; include as many as you can think of.

Now highlight the ones that *actually matter to you*. They might be important because they affect your work or cause problems in your personal life. For example, if you're not a good listener, and that leads your children to think you don't care about what they have to say, then you'll probably want to work at becoming a better listener. Or, if part of your job involves data analysis, which you are not very good at, you could learn to do it better and ask a colleague who is good at it to check your work.

You can't make your weaknesses into strengths. However, with a bit of effort you can usually become 'good enough' at something that's important to you, even if by definition it remains a 'weakness'.

9. OVERDONE STRENGTHS

Our strengths are great assets to us. However, sometimes they can become weaknesses, or at least trip us up, if we overdo them. For example, someone who is great at analysing situations might come across as picking things apart to an extent that they're seen as overly negative.

Which of your strengths do you sometimes overplay, such that they become weaknesses and cause you or others problems?

Being aware of when we overdo our strengths can stop this from becoming a problem in two ways:

1. You are more aware of it so it's less likely to trip you up.

2. You can tell people so that they don't perceive what you're doing as a negative thing. It helps them understand you and your intentions better and saves them from getting annoyed or upset.

Write down any overdone strengths that can become weaknesses below:

_____

_____

MY STRENGTHS MAP

We've looked at your strengths, and the chances are you already were aware of some of them.

We've explored weaknesses and looked at overdone strengths. Bringing all of these together in one visual is handy. You might want to copy the resulting 'Strengths Map' and stick it above your desk as a reminder to keep using those strengths... and to give you a boost when you're having a bad day.

Fill in the boxes below – either by writing or, if you prefer, with pictures.

Notice that there is more space for strengths. As you've probably realized by now, the most benefit comes from focusing your attention on your strengths. Remember, you will only excel by capitalizing on your strengths, not by attempting to fix your weaknesses.

Realized strengths	Previously unrecognized strengths
Strengths I sometimes overdo	**Weaknesses**

Once you've filled in your Strengths Map, try the following exercise: Imagine the map is on the floor. Visualize the four squares. Go and stand inside each square and spend a couple of minutes there with your eyes closed. Start with weaknesses, then move to overdone strengths, then to previously unrecognized strengths, and finally to realized strengths.

Just stand there and mentally get in touch with the things you have written in each square. Write down your responses to the following three questions below:

What's that like?

_____

_____

_____

Is there a difference in the effect each square has on you?

_____

_____

_____

What is that difference?

_____

_____

_____

You may notice when you stand thinking about your weaknesses or overdone strengths you don't feel that great. In contrast, when you're thinking about your strengths, that feels pretty good. It might put a smile on your face and make you feel more energetic and upbeat. You might even notice your body posture changing.

Now you have done some concerted thinking about your strengths, you should be feeling good about yourself. At this point you have a choice. If you want to carry on learning about yourself, and have a go at more exercises that will help you delve into things like your values, turn to page 120. Or, if you'd prefer to learn about how you can apply your strengths to various parts of your life, go to page 82.

Now go to page 142 and complete your Strengths Profile using the insight you've gained about yourself so far.

IN SUMMARY

Knowing your strengths can change your life. Once you are clear about what you are naturally good at and love doing, decision-making about career and study choices becomes much easier. It also gives you an enormous boost in confidence.

Working through this section means you now have a Strengths Profile that you have written yourself after a good deal of in-depth thinking. Your profile on page 142 is therefore a great description of the real you, expressed in your own words.

PART THREE

DEVELOPING
YOUR
STRENGTHS

"Your strengths are the best of you. They magnify what is great about you. You grow and develop the most in the areas of your strengths."

Knowing your strengths is important, but it's not enough. To be as effective and fulfilled as you can be you need to actually *apply* your strengths to your life.

This section answers the following questions:

- How can you develop your strengths?
- What can you do about your weaknesses?
- Where do your skills and knowledge come in?

KEY FACTS
- The most common answer to the question, "Why did you take your current job?" is, "Because it was a great opportunity to do more of what I like to do". On the other hand, "More money" comes in second.
- When asked what their ideal job is, some 60% of the workforce say it's either what they are doing now with more responsibility, or a subset of what they are doing now.
- Approximately 50% say they feel an emotional high at work (a sign they are playing to their strengths) about once a week[6].

This suggests that people out there are already in jobs where they are at least using their strengths some of the time. Does that sound like you, in your current position? If it does, would you like to find a way to use your strengths more of the time? If it doesn't, would you like help finding your strengths and using them more effectively? This section will help you do just that.

WHAT HAPPENS WHEN YOU KNOW YOUR STRENGTHS?

When people become really clear about what their strengths are they often become more motivated and settled just because of that knowledge. Knowing our strengths allows us to understand more clearly why we are happy in certain situations and not in others. And that allows us to actively seek out those situations. This is demonstrated in the examples on page 16.

1. WHY DEVELOP YOUR STRENGTHS?

We grow and develop more in the areas of our strengths because biologically it's significantly more difficult to develop new synaptic connections in the brain. The brain grows more where the synapses are already strong.

The challenge is to increase the time we spend using our strengths, uncovering those we're unaware of, developing these strengths and then adding necessary skills and knowledge so that our capabilities and work satisfaction shoot up.

We all have weaknesses because we are human and we can't be good at everything. The key is to focus attention on the weaknesses that affect us the most and work on minimizing their impact.

I am not advocating ignoring weaknesses but, as we have seen, our weaknesses are not the area of greatest growth potential.

As you grow you become more of who you are. A focus on your strengths means you consciously focus on becoming the very best you can be.

2. HOW TO DEVELOP YOUR STRENGTHS

The great thing about developing our strengths is that it's not complicated and we tend to become even more energized as we are developing them. It's a very different experience from trying to fix weaknesses, which can be draining.

Here's a simple strategy for developing your strengths:

Awareness – Know what your strengths are in the first place. Make sure you ask others for feedback on these so that you uncover any hidden strengths you may not be aware of.

Application – Think about where you are applying your strengths in your life and how often.

Amplify – Look at how and when you could increase the use of your strengths.

Add to – Remember that your strengths are the 'raw material' that makes you who you are. To really excel you need to have knowledge as well as skills.

We'll come back to applying this strategy to different areas of our lives throughout this section.

3. HOW STRENGTHS WORK TOGETHER

Strengths aren't isolated things that operate individually. They work together. And when they do, it's like turbo-charging our performance.

For example, as we discussed earlier, a nurse whose strengths include caring about others, having high standards and wanting to make a difference will stand up for what is right, even though she may not be a naturally assertive person. This combination of strengths means she cannot help but do these things. This demonstrates how powerful it is to look at strengths as a whole and not just individually.

Another example might be a sales person who is very competitive and determined, has a strong drive to achieve their goals and quickly moves on after setbacks. You start to see how these strengths mean they stay motivated to achieve their targets and don't give up or become discouraged by rejection when customers say no to them.

How do your strengths combine to turbo-boost your performance?
Make a note below.

4. HOW STRENGTHS MITIGATE WEAKNESSES

We can use our strengths to help mitigate our weaknesses. Here's an example. Let's imagine that you know you're not very good at data analysis, but you need to complete an important spreadsheet every month for work. If determination and doing the right thing are some of your strengths, then these will help to motivate you to prepare the spreadsheet as well as you can, and perhaps ask a colleague to check it.

Let's look at another example. You might not be a very organized person, but if you have high standards and care a lot about doing the right thing those strengths will help you to become sufficiently organized that it doesn't become a problem.

Now you can see that our strengths can help mitigate our weaknesses and help motivate us to find workable ways around our weaknesses.

5. SKILLS AND KNOWLEDGE

Our strengths are our raw materials. We also need knowledge and skills to perform most of the things we do, and to do them better. For example, we may be good at writing but we need to understand the skills and techniques of editing in order to produce excellent pieces of work.

As another example, someone might have the natural strengths to be a barista in a coffee shop – they might love to connect with people and enjoy working with others. But unless they learn about coffee – the craft of preparing a perfectly steamed macchiato – they can never be excellent at their job.

Your knowledge and skills are your 'ticket to the game' but it's your strengths that lead to excellence.

6. USING YOUR STRENGTHS IN DIFFERENT AREAS OF LIFE

This section answers these questions:

- How can you use your knowledge of strengths in your work or studies?
- How can you apply your strengths to have positive relationships?
- How can you use your strengths to create a happy retirement?

Once you understand your strengths you can bring them to bear in all situations in your life. In this next section we are going to look at how you can do this.

Let's start with something that probably applies to us all – using strengths to build your personal impact.

We've already talked about:

- Understanding how your strengths combine to make you even more effective at what you do.

- Using your strengths to help mitigate your weaknesses.
- Developing your core strengths.
- Adding knowledge and skill to your strengths to build your capabilities.

There are other things you can do too.

An easy one is to keep remembering and consciously using your strengths. This way you maximize your impact by ensuring you use your strengths often and well.

Here are some other simple things you can do:

- Print out your Strengths Profile and stick it above your desk.
- Review your just-completed week every Friday and think about when you used your strengths – in which situations and how often. Make note of this. You could start a personal 'Strengths Book'.
- Last thing at night, or first thing in the morning, spend a minute or two thinking about what you were grateful for the day before. Some of these things might be related to your strengths, others won't. What this exercise does is gets you focused on the positive.

When you keep your strengths in mind it becomes easier to use them consciously, and purposefully, and you feel even stronger. Greater self-confidence inevitably follows.

Keeping your strengths in mind and actively developing them is key to increasing your personal impact. It is also a way to help you keep going when things get tough.

7. THE FOUR A'S STRATEGY

The Four A's strategy will help you to develop and make the most of your strengths.

a. **Awareness.** Think about where you use your strengths in your life. You might want to ask others to help you with this, as they may well see strengths that you don't. (Make notes in the box below...)

b. Application. Now ask yourself how exactly your strengths help you. Be as specific as you possibly can.

c. Amplify. Now think about where else you could use your strengths – in what circumstances, with whom and when.

d. **Add to.** Our strengths are the 'raw materials' that make us who we are. We also need knowledge and skills in order to do certain things well. What skills and knowledge do you need to acquire to make the most of your strengths?

IN SUMMARY

Once we know our strengths we can use them more consciously and in more situations. We can also improve our capability by learning new knowledge and skills.

PART FOUR

APPLYING YOUR STRENGTHS

THIS SECTION ANSWERS THE FOLLOWING QUESTIONS:

- Why and how do you let others know about your strengths?
- Practically speaking, how can your strengths help you?
- How can you apply your strengths in your work, life and relationships?

KEY FACTS

- People who use their strengths every day are six times more likely to feel engaged at work[7].
- Happy couples focus on each other's strengths[8].
- Children learn and grow better when they put their energy into what they 'can' do rather than what they struggle to do[7].

SIGNALING YOUR STRENGTHS TO OTHERS

Letting others know our strengths is a really helpful thing to do for a couple of reasons – if we're working with people it's good to know what contribution others can make. It also saves misunderstandings in communication.

People tend to judge us by our behaviour. That's all they've got to go on. They can't do anything else unless they genuinely know our intentions and our strengths. We judge ourselves by our motivations and intentions but we judge others by their behaviour. And so, unless we know their intentions we can misinterpret their actions.

For example, if you are really interested in people your tendency is probably to ask them lots of questions. This can come across as if you're interrogating them. To avoid annoying them you can say something like, "I hope you don't mind me asking you lots of questions. I'm a curious person and am so interested in other people's lives." This reveals your intention and helps avoid any misunderstanding.

1. PLANNING TO USE YOUR STRENGTHS IN EVERYDAY LIFE

Most people are more likely to get things done if they deliberately plan to do them. It's the same with strengths. Having a weekly 'Strengths Plan' helps keep strengths front-of-mind and makes it more likely that we'll use them. It also can help us to get things done that we find challenging.

In the table opposite, list the major things you know you will be doing in the week ahead, and really try to put some thought into it:

(a) Which of my strengths will help me?
(b) What else will help me?
(c) Is there anyone else who could help me?

At the end of each day or week think about how well it went and what you could do next time to use your strengths even more. Examples have been provided to guide you.

Activities this week	Which of my strengths will help me	How	Reflection
Project meeting	*Organizing, conscientiousness, taking responsibility, making a difference*	*We have to get a lot done so I will prepare an agenda and circulate it well in advance. I will suggest I lead the meeting. I've been putting this off.*	

2. USING AND DEVELOPING YOUR STRENGTHS AT WORK

"It doesn't matter what the job is – if you're the right person for it, you're serving others, and yourself."

Let's apply the Four A's strategy on page 76 to using and developing your strengths at work:

a. **Awareness.** Think about where you use your strengths in your current role or in your studies. If possible, ask co-workers or friends to help you with this as they may well see strengths that you don't. Make a note below. Examples have been given in italics.

> *I love to connect with new people. This helps me get various stakeholders on board when we start new projects. It also makes it easy for me to engage potential new clients when I meet them at events.*

b. Application. Now ask yourself how exactly your strengths help you. Be as specific as you possibly can.

My strength in connecting means I talk to people, ask them questions and we each end up feeling that connection. It means we stay in touch, so it opens up the possibility of working together longer-term.

c. Amplify. Now think about where else you could use your strengths – in what circumstances, with whom and when.

I could go to more professional events, including ones I haven't been to before. Knowing I connect well with people I could go places where influential, senior-level people are and connect with them to further my purpose. I could find out who my colleagues would like to connect with and go along to meet these people with them.

d. **Add to.** As we've seen, our strengths are the 'raw materials' that make us who we are. We still need knowledge and skills to add to the strengths and give us real competence. So, what skills and knowledge could you learn that would make you even more capable? Are there any projects or tasks that you could volunteer for to develop your strengths, or to use strengths that you are not currently using? And do you have colleagues who are strong where you are weak so you can swap these tasks for mutual benefit?

> *I could learn how to do webinars so I can connect more easily with people in other locations. I could also improve my Spanish so I can connect better with more people in our Spanish client organization.*

2.1 THINKING ABOUT YOUR PERFORMANCE

Have you ever found yourself having the same discussion year after year in performance reviews, where the focus is on what you need to be better at? The same thing comes up the following year and, no matter what you do, nothing seems to change.

It's likely that the thing you are not very good at is not a natural strength or interest so you always struggle with it. There might be marginal gain by consistently plugging away at trying to be better at it. In the end, though, spending time and energy deploying your strengths to your best advantage would be time better spent.

SOME QUESTIONS TO ASK YOURSELF:
- How can I expand my job to make more use of my strengths?
- Are there any projects that excite me and in which I'd like to be involved that would allow me to use my strengths more?
- Is there something new I can try, to see whether I like it and it's suited to my strengths (those I know about already and ones I don't know about)?

"Work is a huge part of your life, so you may as well do something you love… or at least that comes naturally to you. Why would you go through life spending 60-70% of that life not enjoying your work and struggling?"

3. USING YOUR STRENGTHS TO GET A NEW JOB

Knowing your strengths can save you from embarking on a career path or taking a job that you wouldn't be suited to or happy in. Sometimes people decide at quite a young age on a career path without giving a lot of thought as to whether it would make them happy or be right for them. For instance, a young journalist might have an ambition to work his way up to becoming a managing editor. He may well have the strengths needed, but he may not. It's very possible that he loves finding a story and writing, but he might not be the type of person who's comfortable with being in charge. To be a great managing editor you need to love being in charge.

It's actually quite common for organizations to promote people into management positions because they are good at their job, but it ends up being a disaster because they don't like managing or are not very good at it. Usually both. The value of knowing yourself and your strengths cannot be overstated. It can save from you making career decisions that could make you really unhappy.

Have you ever been promoted into a job where you were a square peg in a round hole?

What was that like?

What career moves are you thinking about now?

To what extent do you think such a move would allow you to play to your strengths, succeed and be fulfilled in your professional life?

PREPARING YOUR CV

Traditional CVs focus on experience and achievements. This is important information for a prospective employer. However, it doesn't give a great sense of the kind of person you are beyond things like good team player, excellent communicator, self-starter. Lots of people put these things on their CVs. They are hackneyed terms and vague labels that don't make you stand out from the pack.

As you become more aware of your strengths you'll find that you can write a better description of yourself. In a short paragraph you should be able to give the reader a much better idea of what you're like as a person. Below is an example of such a paragraph. This person has put this in a 'Personal Statement', which should always appear on the front page of a CV. It helps prospective employers get an idea of the kind of person she is because she's describing her strengths and what motivates her.

I am extremely good at making the most out of any situation and approaching challenges with a positive attitude. I am an adaptable person and I love taking on responsibility. I'm curious and learn quickly. I'm also conscientious and have always had a strong work ethic. I love working with others and get on well with people of all ages and from all walks of life.

This gives the reader a good idea of what she is like as a person beyond the usual career history, work experience and qualifications included in a CV. It brings her to life on the page!

STRENGTHS-BASED INTERVIEWS, AND HOW TO PREPARE FOR THESE

Strengths-based interviews are becoming more common and I am sometimes asked how to prepare for them. One of the reasons organizations like strengths-based interviews is that it's difficult to prepare for them, so they yield much more genuine and natural answers than competency-based interviewing, where candidates can intuitively trot out the 'right' answer. Strengths-based interviews are a lot more difficult to fake and they are genuinely two-way. The interviewers learn about you as a person – what you're naturally good at, what energizes you and what you enjoy. You find out whether you will be a good fit for the organization.

The best advice I can offer is not to be afraid to be yourself and let your individuality shine through. That is what the interviewers want from you.

SHARING STRENGTHS IN A TRADITIONAL INTERVIEW

Have you ever had the experience of leaving an interview feeling that the interviewers didn't get to know you well enough or didn't give you a chance to shine, or both? Then, if they didn't offer you the job, it felt unfair because you weren't given the opportunity to show how good you are. And if you were offered a position, you may have worried that they shouldn't have offered it because they didn't find out enough to know whether you actually weren't a very good candidate. So, what can you do if you have interviewers who are not asking you questions that give you an opportunity to show you at your best? Here are some tips:

- Before you go in to the interview, be clear on which of your strengths you want them to know about. Obviously choose those that demonstrate that you'll be good at the job. Think about what you want to say about those strengths.

- If the interview is a competency-based one – where they ask you questions like, "Tell me about a time when you had to overcome a difficulty" – you can tell them about overcoming a challenge but also take the opportunity to mention what strengths you used. For example, you can say something like, "That came quite naturally to me because I'm a determined person and one of my strengths is always achieving what I set out to do."

- Find opportunities in the interview to highlight your strengths. It's not all that difficult. For example, use phrases like, "I'm known for being really good at developing others", "One of my top strengths is being analytical", "What makes me a good [whatever they have asked you about] is these strengths [and tell them what the strengths are]". If you're having a hard time finding an opportunity to tell them about your strengths, you can try saying, "If you were to ask me what my main strengths are, I'd tell you [and tell them]".

- Send a brief follow-up email telling the interviewers how much you enjoyed meeting them, and how enthusiastic you are about the role and the organization. Summarize in brief bullets what you think makes you a good match for the job and the contribution you think you can make.

GETTING OFF TO A GOOD START IN YOUR JOB

There are huge benefits to having had an interview where the interviewers get to know you and your strengths. First, *you* know that *they* know what you're like and that you're right for the job. So, you're not left with any nagging doubts that they made the wrong decision hiring you, which can happen if you don't feel like they got to know you very well in the interview. The second is that your new employer knows a lot more about you than they would have through a traditional interview. This means they can motivate and recognize you in ways that matter to you, assigning you to projects that play to your strengths and ultimately having meaningful development conversations with you.

All this will help give you a confident start to your new job. And it means you can really take ownership of your own development and career growth because you know what you're good at and energized by, so can stretch yourself in those directions.

You will also be able to look for ways to use strengths you're not getting a chance to use in your current job, as well as think about potential future roles where you'll have the chance to play to your strengths even more.

4. THE STRENGTHS APPROACH FOR LEADERS

Some questions for consideration:

- How many of the people you directly manage or influence do you know so well that it's easy for you to get the best out of them and motivate them?
- How long does it normally take you to get to know people well enough to do that?
- Would you like to speed up that process?

Imagine knowing your team so well that it's really easy to manage, motivate and develop them. It would be almost like having a 'user-manual' for each person that tells you how to work with them and get the best from them.

That's what knowing your people's strengths can do for you. And if you assign individuals to jobs based on their strengths you will have a lot of good insight into them.

Try it. This is a surprisingly simple but powerful approach because:

- You are showing that you understand and are interested in them.
- Your employees will be very motivated by these discussions simply because you are talking to them about their strengths.
- You are getting them to think in very specific and positive terms about their performance and development.
- You are treating them as responsible colleagues who want to contribute in a way that's a win for them and a win for the organization.
- You are having a conversation about how they can contribute more in a way that is energizing and exciting to them, not in a way that makes them feel put-upon.

This will not only enable your people to perform well and achieve their potential, it will also make your life as a leader easier and more fulfilling.

Having said that, you don't want to be pie-in-sky about this. The reality is that we can't all spend 100% of our time playing to our strengths and doing what energizes us. In fact, very few of us have the luxury of being able to do that. So you *will* need to help your people to be good enough at the things that are their weaknesses or that they don't like doing.

As a manager, though, do you ever find yourself doing any of these things?

- Expecting people to enjoy doing the bits of the job that you relish.
- Expecting them to be good at tasks that you're good at, and becoming frustrated when they're not.

- Noticing and focusing on what the person is not so good at rather than putting your main focus on what they are good at.
- Not recognizing when someone's annoying behaviour is actually indicative of an overdone strength. For example, someone who has very high standards might come across as nitpicking when they obsess over high standards.
- Not asking someone's reasoning when their behaviour annoys you, when it's likely that they had the best of intentions.
- Pushing someone to do things that you know, or suspect, they're not very good at.

All of this can mean unnecessary frustrations as well as demotivated employees and performance that is not as good as it could be.

So, here are some simple tips and techniques for productively approaching the points listed above.

Instead of this...	Try this...
Thinking that people will enjoy and be good at the bits of the job you relish and are good at	Work out how you are different and make sure the things that are important to you get done by talking to the person about how they can accomplish them, or getting someone else to do them
Noticing and focusing on what the person is not so good at	Remember all their strengths (which you may take for granted). Talk to them about how their strengths can help them overcome their weaknesses, and how to become better in the areas that are not being done well enough
Not noticing when someone's annoying behaviour is indicative of a strength	Next time someone does something, or behaves in a way you find annoying, think about what strength it could be a result of. This can make you switch from annoyed to appreciative. Really!
Focusing on the behaviour instead of the intention	Before you 'react' to someone's behaviour, think about what their positive intention might have been. In fact, you can ask them outright. Also remember that others will inevitably judge you by your behaviour because they can't see your intent. If you think your actions might prompt a negative response, try positioning what you're about to do or say like this: "In commenting on your proposal I'll be very honest and straightforward because I want to help you make it the best it can possibly be."
Asking a person to do something that you know they're not very good at	Explain why you're asking them, and be honest. Maybe there is no one else to do it. Maybe you want them to give it a go to see whether they can improve. Acknowledge that you know it's not one of their strengths and that they don't particularly love doing it

5. USING YOUR STRENGTHS IN YOUR STUDIES

Studying what you're interested in is pretty important. Studying can be hard work, so choosing subjects you enjoy will help you stay motivated through the tough times.

To get you into the swing of thinking about what you are drawn to, give some thought to these questions:

- Which programmes do you love to watch on TV?
- Which do you always turn off? (In my case it's the gardening programmes!)
- Which links on Twitter, Facebook, LinkedIn, etc. do you click on?

What themes emerge from your media habits? Are you drawn to hearing about people's lives, to history, to environmental issues? What attracts your attention and really draws you in?

Now, take a look at the subjects you're studying (or are thinking of studying). Put a tick in the box that best applies to each one.

List all the subjects you're studying	Love this subject	It's OK	Really don't like it

List the subjects that you love below and make note of what really appeals to you about each one.

Can you see any commonalities or themes emerging? Jot them down here.

Now think about other subjects that appeal to you – ones that you haven't studied before or don't know anything about. The reason for doing this is so that you don't narrow your horizons too much.

You should now have an idea of all the subjects that you know you are interested in, and those you may be interested in and want to explore at some point in the future, even if it's just as a hobby.

The next thing to think about is your natural strengths, motivators and values – all the things you discovered about yourself in Part Two. There are a couple of key things to think about relative to your studies:

1. To what extent will the subjects you choose to study allow you to play to your interests and use your strengths?

2. How can your strengths help you to study well and enjoy your time studying?

6. USING STRENGTHS IN PARENTING

Knowing your child's strengths, values and motivators is like having a personalized parenting manual. Knowing about and applying strengths-based thinking can make a big difference if your child:

- **Lacks confidence or self-esteem**
  Knowing they have strengths in the first place can be a big revelation for some young people. Knowing what they are and being appreciated for them can change the way they think and feel about themselves. They can go from having very low self-esteem to being quite confident just by understanding their strengths. As a parent this allows you to encourage them to use their strengths and keep them focused on those rather than slipping back into an emphasis on what they think they are no good at.

- **Is unlike you so you find it hard to relate to them**
  It's hard for any of us to relate to people who are unlike us. When it's our children it can be baffling and frustrating for all concerned. If you're a parent who is naturally optimistic, and your child is very analytical and spots flaws in things, that can come across to you as not being positive. You may find yourself constantly trying to get them to see the bright side of things.

That can be annoying to an analytical person – not because they don't want to see the bright side, but because they feel at home when they're in analysis mode.

- **Has difficulty making choices**
  It's impossible to help someone to make good life choices without knowledge of who they really are, deep down. Without this knowledge, you could be inadvertently encouraging them to live someone else's life!

HOW DO YOU ENCOURAGE YOUR CHILD IN THE DIRECTION OF THEIR STRENGTHS WITHOUT PIGEONHOLING THEM OR 'NARROWING' THEM?

It helps to encourage your child to try new things so that they discover more about themselves and what they love. The more they can discover their true nature and go in that direction, the more fulfilled they will be. As with anything, you just need to be careful not to limit them through pigeonholing. Encourage them to try new things, ask them what exactly appeals to them about the things they love, listen to them carefully and inspire them to keep trying new things... and discover more about themselves.

WHAT PRACTICAL DIFFERENCE CAN A STRENGTHS APPROACH MAKE TO CHILDREN?

Teach children about the concept of strengths, encourage them to stretch themselves in the direction of their strengths and encourage them to try anything that they are drawn to. Whether they like a given activity or not, encourage them to reflect on what they like and don't like. Ask them questions like:

- What was it like to do that?
- What did you like about it?
- What made you happy about it?
- What other things do you like doing and get excited by?
- If you didn't like it, what was it that you didn't like?
- Are there parts that you liked?

Children can get annoyed when they're bombarded by too many questions at once, but asking one or two of these will help you to help them sort through which activities energize them. And that will steer them towards things that they may want to do more of.

An example of how this can help is Dan. He is 11 and loves dance. His parents have been taking him to dance classes every week for several years and were so happy that he'd found something that lit him up. Suddenly, however, he decided he didn't want to go anymore and all that they could get out of him was, "I don't like it." When they asked him about whether there were any bits that he did like or hadn't liked, and what was happening in class on the days he enjoyed, they made an important discovery. They learned that Dan loved breakdancing because of its free, improvisational nature. All the other styles of dance were tightly choreographed and he found that too constraining. Had they not explored this with him, they would have consigned dancing to the 'don't like it anymore' category and their son would have given it up altogether. By searching around for the thing that he loved they found him a breakdancing group, and Dan dances in every spare moment he has!

BEWARE OF LIMITING BELIEFS

Someone I know told his 18-year-old daughter not to expect to get a job that she loved because most people don't like their jobs! She read about strengths and challenged him on his view. Thank goodness she did. My work involves helping organizations select people who are a great fit for the work they do. Having worked with all sorts of people from all walks of life, I know that it definitely IS possible to be in a job you love, whether you're a caterer, a barista, a scientist, whatever. We all have strengths and we all have things we come alive doing.

7. USING STRENGTHS IN RELATIONSHIPS

Understanding another person's strengths can help any relationship to thrive in a number of ways:

- **It makes us appreciate the other person and avoid incorrect assumptions about them.** This is especially true if the person has a strength that we didn't see as a strength, or that we might have found annoying! For example, if someone has a strength in being productive and lives his life by lists, he gets lots done because he tears through his lists of things to do with great relish. If his wife doesn't have this strength it might cause problems at weekends because she feels he prefers doing tasks to just spending time with her and their children. Having learned about each other's strengths, she appreciates the fact that he does lots for her because he puts the jobs she wants him to do in his list. But she might also discover that she can get him to put activities with her and the kids on his list, which means they'll get done, and that meets her needs too!

- **It means we're less judgmental of others.** I'll admit I used to get frustrated with people before I knew about strengths. "Why can't they just do x properly?" I sometimes thought to myself.

At times, I'd find myself focusing on what they couldn't do instead of what they did very well. Nowadays I can easily spot people's strengths and I focus on appreciating those. And when I find someone annoying I ask myself whether it could be a manifestation of an overdone strength. Quite often it is, and that generates more appreciation for what they have rather than angst over what they lack.

- **It means we can work better as a team.** When we're in any kind of relationship with someone, having different strengths means you can help and support each other by 'filling in' for each other. For example, if one of you is very detail-oriented and the other takes in the big picture, that adds richness to discussions and makes for better decision-making.

- **It can give you greater appreciation for yourself.** If you have strengths that others don't they may rely on you to contribute those strengths and that can make you feel good about yourself and the contribution you make. And that, in turn, makes you feel valued.

WE JUDGE OURSELVES ON OUR INTENTIONS BUT OTHERS ON THEIR BEHAVIOUR

A person's strengths drive their behaviour. For example, if someone is great at spotting and solving problems, the way that shows itself is to point out what is wrong and offer solutions. This could be annoying if you just want someone to listen to you rather than telling you how you could solve the problem. Knowing that problem solving is one of their strengths and knowing that their intention is to help you goes a long way to reducing annoyance.

Just as we judge others on their behaviour, they judge us. Clarifying, or signaling, our intention helps create better understanding. All you have to do is precede what you say with words like, "I am hoping to be helpful so I'll play devil's advocate with your idea", or "If that's not what you want, just tell me". That way they know that you are trying to help, and not thoughtlessly criticize.

WHAT IF SOMEONE'S WEAKNESSES CAUSE YOU PROBLEMS?

Focus on appreciating other people's strengths, not their weaknesses. But they may have weaknesses that affect you, in which case talk to the person and tell them the impact their behaviour has on you. The key is not to criticize, and to talk about the behaviour instead of the person. For example, out of two business partners, one was an excellent listener and the other wasn't. Occasionally there was an embarrassing situation with customers because the person who couldn't listen well would misrepresent customers' problems in proposals. The business partners agreed to check their understanding before sending a proposal off to a client. They also figured out that at times it was anxiety that prevented them from listening because they were worried about not knowing what to say next.

So, understanding strengths and recognizing that we all have weaknesses can make for easier, non-confrontational conversations.

8. USING STRENGTHS IN RETIREMENT

If you are coming close to retirement, what do you think about it?

- Are you worried about what you will do when you retire?
- Are you worried that you will miss certain aspects of your working life?
- Do you wonder 'who' you will be once you have left your work identity behind?
- Are you looking forward to leaving behind a job you've never really loved?
- Are you excited about the free time you will have to spend on things you really like doing?
- Are you looking forward to discovering new interests?

Whatever your thoughts and feelings are about retirement, clearly understanding your strengths and what makes you happy will help make sure you are fulfilled.

IS 'RETIREMENT' THE RIGHT WORD?

I don't think it is the right word. The dictionary definition is 'the act or fact of leaving one's job and ceasing work'. It doesn't suggest a transition to a new purpose in life. In fact, many people still do, or want to do, lots of things. The traditional three-part life – education, work, retirement – is not the experience many people have or want to have. I will use the word 'retirement' for ease of reference here but I prefer to think of the end of formal employment as a time for creating a portfolio of activities that a person enjoys, finds rewarding and, indeed, an opportunity to earn some money if that's what they want or need.

HOW ONE MAN PLAYED TO HIS STRENGTHS IN RETIREMENT

Gerry was in his 50s when he took retirement. He had been a senior manager in a number of jobs he loved. He started his career in the Merchant Navy, which he chose partly because he wanted to travel. He loved travelling and had done so all his life. In some ways he was looking forward to retiring, but in other ways he was very worried about what it would be like. He just couldn't imagine a life without urgent and pressing things to do. Here's what he was worrying about:

- He loved to be in charge and felt that when he retired he would be in charge of nothing much.
- He was worried about not being able to travel as extensively as he had.
- He knew his identity was closely associated with who he was at work.

Gerry hadn't previously thought about his strengths, values and what motivated him. He just considered himself lucky to have fallen into a job that suited him well. When he started to work out what he was really like, what was important to him and what energized him he started to come up with all sorts of ideas of things he wanted to do. He knew he was a good leader and he loved being in charge, so he volunteered to set up a local youth club in the village where he lived. No one had managed to get such a service off the ground before. Under Gerry's leadership the youth club is now thriving and it helps not only young people but others who volunteer and find it very rewarding work. Gerry knew nothing about young people and what they needed, but one of his strengths is curiosity and learning. And he also loves to make a difference. He's also a courageous person with a strong sense of justice. He took on a non-executive directorship on a board that was rife with conflict and strong characters. Gerry relished the challenge of helping this team become much more positive and high-performing. He was happy to confront issues that others had shied away from. After less than a year Gerry was as busy as he'd ever been when he was working full time. And he likes it that way. He's very happy and fulfilled, particularly because he's making a difference on a broader platform than he was.

Some people are lucky and manage to create a new kind of life that suits them well without ever knowing anything about strengths. There are probably more people who flounder, though, and struggle to find contentment in retirement.

PLANNING FOR A FULFILLED RETIREMENT

If you're thinking of retiring in the next few years here are some questions to ask yourself.

- How do I want my life to be in five, ten, twenty years' time?
    - ◊ What kind of things do I want to fill my day with?
    - ◊ Who do I want to see regularly?
    - ◊ Where would I like to be living?

- What kinds of things do I want to fill my time doing?
    - ◊ What kinds of things do I want to do that I can't currently do?
    - ◊ What would I like to try that I've never tried?

- Who do I want to be around?
    - ◊ Who do I want to see more of?
    - ◊ Who do I want to keep in touch with from my working life?
    - ◊ Are there any new types of people I would like to meet and make friends with?
    - ◊ Are there certain people who I'd rather not be around so often?

In order to answer these questions in a meaningful way you need to know yourself fairly well. That means knowing what you love doing, what energizes you, what's important to you and what really motivates you.

Alison was coming up to retirement. She had a very busy job where she worked long hours. She had a small group of friends but didn't see much of them because she was always so busy. She also had let her hobbies slide because her work was so demanding. If she wasn't careful her retirement would feel like a void. She would go from not having enough hours in the day to not having enough to do to fill her time. She needed to do some serious thinking about what her future – the rest of her life – would look like.

Thinking ahead was essential for Alison if she was to avoid the sudden shock of stopping work and having nothing to do. It also meant she started to think of possibilities and look forward to retirement.

For some people, retirement provides them with the opportunity to use their strengths more than ever.

Do you think you have the opportunity to do what you do well every day at work?

If the answer to this is no, then retirement is an opportunity to use your strengths to a greater degree and, in so doing, enrich your life. And I'm not just talking about spending more time on your hobbies, though you might do that too. If you get to know your strengths and what motivates you, you may well find other hobbies.

Robert knew he loved a challenge and had always been someone who strived to be the best he could be. He'd played golf for years, which fitted in well with these strengths. One thing he hadn't thought about before was playing Bridge. He thought he might like it because it's a partnership game – he'd always enjoyed that aspect of golf. He has a good memory and always liked maths, although he'd never had the opportunity to pursue his interest in maths in his work. Bridge ticked that box for him and he loves it.

Use your strengths to stay young at heart throughout your life.

Doing what you love, having a purpose and enjoying the small things in life will help you to stay fulfilled and young at heart.

List here all the things you love to do – even the small things: people watching, enjoying a coffee in your local café, browsing in book shops, chatting to the neighbours. Keep this list and make sure you do the small things you love as much as possible.

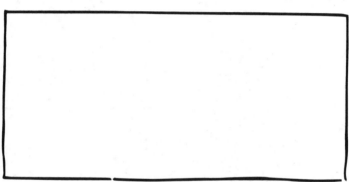

Each night before you go to bed list the things you did that day that you love. And the next morning write down what you were grateful for from the day before. This 'gratitude journal' idea really does work and has been proven to improve psychological health and satisfaction with life.

IN SUMMARY
In Part Four we've looked at putting your strengths into practice. We've looked at how you can actively and consciously use your strengths in different aspects of your life. There are insights and practical tips on applying your strengths to different parts of your life – work, getting a job, studying, parenting, relationships and retirement.

PART FIVE

WHAT ELSE DO YOU NEED TO BE FULFILLED?

"Really knowing what makes you tick is so important and hardly ever talked about at school or at work!"

THIS SECTION ANSWERS THE FOLLOWING QUESTIONS

- What factors, other than strengths, will enable you to thrive at work and in life?
- What are some common stumbling blocks and how can you overcome them?
- What kind of support could you seek from others?

You now have a really good idea of your strengths and how to apply them. However that's not enough. In order to be the absolute best that we can be we need to be motivated and actively engaged in doing things that are important to us, so that our life has meaning. We also need to be able to deal with the tricky things in life that can trip us up, like the way we respond to challenging situations. Along the way, all of us need help, so we will be taking a look at who you can find to help you and in what ways.

KEY FACTS

- Studies show that money increases happiness when it takes people from a situation where there are real threats, like poverty or homelessness, to circumstances that are reasonably safe. After that money doesn't matter much.

- Research by psychologist Daniel Kahneman showed that money increases happiness until one reaches the $75,000 threshold. After that our emotional wellbeing doesn't increase with additional income[9].

- Research by Stanford University psychologist Jennifer Aaker found that meaningful lives were associated with being a giver rather than a taker. And meaningfulness is about expressing and defining yourself and your purpose[10].

1. WHAT'S IMPORTANT TO YOU?

Your values are the things that are the most important to you. They're the fundamental things you hold true, like fairness, integrity and helping others. Shaped by our family and early-life experiences, they represent the core of who we are and what we stand for.

Values have a major influence on our attitudes and actions. They are also the measures we use for deciding how we feel about other people, our job and the organizations we work for.

Being clear about what's important to you – your values – will help you to make choices that are right for you and that are rewarding. For example, if it's important to you to help other people you will be much more satisfied if this is a central part of the work you do.

A really good way of discovering what your values are is to think about what they're not. Try this exercise:

Imagine that your job is Chief Misery Officer. Your role is to create a workplace, school or university that would be your idea of sheer misery.

Jot down your ideas. What would it be like? What would the people be like? How would they behave? What would you be required to do there on a daily basis? What else would be happening that would lead you to really dislike this place and the work that you were doing there?

Write about it below or draw a picture of it.

How does the idea of this place affect you when you think about it? What does it do to your mood or feelings?

Ok... before you get TOO miserable let's have a look at the opposite of all the things you wrote. In the box on the following page describe your idea of a wonderful workplace. Write about the look and feel of the place, what people are like there, how are they're behaving, what work you're engaged in and why you really and truly love it there.

Looking at your two descriptions – of the miserable place and the happy place – what do they tell you about your values? What do they say about the things that are most important to you?

Next, list your core values. Below are some examples to help you get rolling.

Helpfulness	Honesty	Courage	Respect for
Equality	Independence	Community	others
Learning	Friendship	Harmony	Self-sufficiency
Teamwork	Trust	Family	Status
Adventure	Truth	Self-discipline	Fun
Pleasure	Recognition	Duty	Order
Sense of	Generosity	Loyalty	Freedom
purpose	Fairness	Justice	

In the table below note in your own words the values that are most important to you. These are ones that, if they were infringed or taken away from you, would hurt the most. Then describe what each value looks like in practice in your life. The text in italics is an example.

My core values	How they show in practice
Helpfulness	*At work or home, I like to help others. Whether it's little things like shopping for my elderly neighbour or bigger things like staying at work late to help a stressed colleague, I always look for opportunities to be helpful.*

2. WHAT MOTIVATES YOU?

Our motivations are one of the most important things we can know about ourselves. It's as important to know what motivates us as it is to know our strengths. Why? Because if you're not motivated to do something you won't actually do it (or will do it half-heartedly) no matter what your strengths are.

Our motivators reflect our values and our strengths. They are the driving force behind why we do what we do. They are like the engine inside us. Without motivation, we wouldn't want to get up in the morning. Consider the following questions:

* Have you ever had that feeling where you just can't find the motivation to do something that you are obliged to do? What is that like?
* On the other hand, think of when you are highly motivated to do something. What is that like?
* We need motivation to feel happy and fulfilled, and to get things done. What are your motivations?

Have a look at the motivations below:

Leader
It's important to you to be responsible for others' performance.

Creativity
You want the opportunity to use your imagination and generate new ideas.

Purpose
You want to serve a cause or do work that's important to you.

Stability
You need to feel secure in your job and work.

Specialist
You want to achieve mastery in your chosen area.

Status
You like other people to recognize your importance.

Friendship
You like to have close friends in your life.

Ethics
You like to follow certain principles and a moral code.

Balance
It's important to you to have the flexibility to combine work with other areas of your life.

Challenge
You like to test yourself by solving tricky problems.

Personal freedom
You want autonomy to be able to do things your way.

Making a difference
You like to engage in activity that has a positive impact on people or the world.

Material reward
Financial success is important to you.

Pick the top three or four motivators that are the most important to you – the ones that you really couldn't be without. An example is in italics.

My top motivators	Why this is important to me
Making a difference	*Life would seem pointless without this. The things I am most excited about are the things that I do that make the most difference. I would lose energy without them.*

3. WHAT YOU CAN CONTROL AND WHAT YOU CAN'T

If we spend time struggling with something we have no control over, or worrying about it, it can really get in the way of our day-to-day wellbeing.

In any given situation, there are some things we can't control and some things we can. The important thing is to identify what you can and what you can't influence, and then put effort into those things that you can have an impact on. Here's an example:

Emily is struggling with her boss. Some days he is quite reasonable and supportive. Other days he is distant and changes his mind about what he wants. She never knows where she is with him and it's making her frustrated. It's starting to affect her badly as she spends a lot of time worrying about it.

Let's look at what Emily can and cannot control about this situation.

What Emily can't control – Her boss's behaviour, such as whether or not he is supportive, and the fact that he changes his mind a lot.

What she may be able to influence – She might be able to influence him into changing his mind by talking to him on a good day about the goals he'd like her to achieve and agreeing on a detailed plan. It's possible that if she sits him down and gets him to talk it through he may not change his mind later.

What she can control – There are a couple of things Emily has control over. One is how she reacts to this trying situation in the workplace. She can keep on letting it get to her or she can assume an attitude of, 'Oh that's him, and he's not likely to change'. By doing the latter, she'll come to accept him for how he is. Or, of course, she can look for another job.

The point is that we waste energy worrying about things we have little or no control over. It's empowering and makes us more productive if we focus on the things we can actually influence.

Try this for yourself. List below all the concerns or worries you have about a given situation.

Now go back over your list and write next to each item whether it's something you: (a) may be able to influence; (b) have no control over; (c) can definitely do something about.

4. CHOOSING YOUR RESPONSE

If the way we think – particularly in our expectations of our own and others' behaviour – is full of 'shoulds', 'oughts' and 'musts', then we'll almost certainly get annoyed or be disappointed on a regular basis. Our disappointment or anger will then affect our own behaviour and wellbeing.

Here are two tips to alleviate frustration and achieve the end-result you want:

1. Accept that everyone is different, and give up expecting people to behave the way you think they should. It may be that the person's intentions are good even though we found their behaviour difficult. Go back to what you can influence and decide whether it's possible to change their behaviour or not.

2. Understand the types of situations that trigger strong reactions in you. The clearer you are about the things that get to you, the better prepared you will be to manage those situations. Again, remember that we can choose how we react to a situation even if we cannot control that situation.

Write down the types of situations that make you angry, frustrated or nervous. Think about instances where you feel like your emotions are managing you, rather than you managing them. Write down next to each situation how your strengths, values and motivators can help you deal with these challenges. An example appears in italics.

Situations that make me angry or frustrated	How can my strengths, values and motivators help me with this?
My colleague turning up late	*I'm honest and straightforward so I could tell her how that affects me. I care about people so I could ask whether there's something that is making her late.*

Here are some other tips that can help you in such situations. Circle the ones that could work for you.

- Assume that the person has reasons for their actions that have nothing to do with you.
- Decide not to take it personally if someone does something that you find problematic.
- Take a deep breath.
- Count to ten.
- Don't say anything – if someone you're dealing with is in a bad mood just leave them alone.
- Try to put yourself in their shoes.
- Think about what you can do to achieve a positive outcome.

Sometimes something happens and you have time to think about it before you have to respond. If so, the following can help:

- Go for a walk.
- Bring some perspective to the situation. Ask yourself how important it really is in the scheme of things.
- Let off steam by talking through your frustrations with a good friend or colleague.
- Write your thoughts down on paper so that you can get them out of your system.

You may be the type of person who can choose how to react in any situation. If you're not, and you tend to let external factors control how you feel, you now know that this doesn't have to happen. With practice, you can usually decide how to react, whatever comes your way. Feeling in control will make you feel less stressed.

5. YOUR 'TEAM'

Having people who help and support you is very important. Think of your support network as a team, composed of different people who support you in different ways.

Some people find it embarrassing to ask for help from others. They might be worried about appearing unable to cope or they may think they're being a pest. However, in my experience, most people love being asked for help. It's a compliment after all that people think you have something to offer. We've been looking at strengths in this book and some people have strengths in helping others or developing others – for them it's energizing and rewarding to help others!

When you ask for help be clear about the type of support you want. Is it help finding a solution to a problem, do you want their feedback on something, do you want someone to play devil's advocate? Or, maybe, do you just want to test out an idea?

Different people help us in different ways. Write down the people in your life who help you. Think of friends, family, neighbours, people at work, even the man in the corner shop – anyone at all who helps you in however small a way. Also think about people who *could* help you but you've never thought of them that way in the past.

In the box below, write down the names of those you could potentially call on for help.

Type of help	Name of person
Someone I can always rely on	
Someone I just enjoy chatting with	
Someone who makes me feel competent, valued and confident	
Someone who is a valuable source of information	
Someone who challenges me	
Someone who introduces me to new people	
Someone who will help me think through a problem	
Someone who makes me feel positive and optimistic	
Someone who gives me constructive feedback	
Someone who doesn't judge me and is always there for me, no matter what	
Someone who just makes me smile or cheers me up when I see them	
Someone who is good at giving me practical help	
Someone who supports me emotionally	

Now that you've plotted out your support network, consider these questions and jot down your thoughts on the following page.

- What do you notice about your network?
- Where do you need to strengthen it?
- Who can help you do this?

IN SUMMARY

This book is about the power of knowing and using strengths. There are some other key factors, though, that make a big difference to our wellbeing and success. We need to know what our values are because they give us a sense of purpose and are those things that are deeply important to us.

Then there are our motivators – the things that are the driving force behind what we do. It's no good having strengths if we're not motivated to do anything with them. We also need to be clear about what to expend our energy on trying to change so that we avoid trying to fix things that are outside of our control.

Finally, we can't thrive unless we have support from others.

CONCLUSION

Having worked in this field for over a decade, I have seen how strengths can change people's lives. For some it's a revelation that they are actually good at some things. Many people I have worked with feel a great deal of emotion, relief and excitement upon realizing that they're just fine as they are, having spent a lifetime trying to mould themselves into something they're not.

Make no mistake, knowing your strengths is powerful.

It can make the difference between a miserable working life and a fulfilling one.

It can help guide young people making choices about studies and careers in which they'll thrive and be happy.

It can turn someone with low self-esteem into a person who values themselves.

And for all of us it is the key to motivation and success.

You can never reach your full potential by trying to fix your weaknesses, only by knowing your strengths and stretching yourself in the direction of your strengths.

I hope that in learning about strengths from this book you've gained insight into yourself that is useful, motivating and affirming, and that you are all set to put this knowledge to work. I wish you all the best in your endeavours.

May you go from strength to strength.

EXAMPLE STRENGTHS PROFILE

Me: Joe Bloggs

My Strengths Profile:
I am a highly self-motivated, resilient individual who thrives on new challenges. My current role and my experience of managing my own business have given me strong people and process management skills. One of my strengths is managing, motivating and engaging with people from multi-disciplinary teams and from all walks of life. I am known for establishing strong and productive long-term relationships with internal and external customers and staff. I have a strong work ethic and am extremely dependable and loyal. In all my roles I have achieved performance levels that others thought impossible in, sometimes, extremely challenging circumstances.

I teach dance to both adults and children and no matter what their individual ability I am able to encourage them to reach their goals.

My best self: themes
Times when I felt very alive and felt a strong sense of satisfaction have been characterized by hardship. It's clear that I'm a very determined person, I don't give up and I care about justice and doing the right thing. Also I get a lot of satisfaction from developing and pushing others to achieve their potential.

My top strengths

I love to be in charge

I keep going when things are tough

I love developing others

It's important to me to do the right thing

I have a strong work ethic

Feedback from others

The main theme that emerged from others' feedback is what a good leader I am, that I am fair and encouraging, and that inspires people to want to do well. Several people said how calm I am, which I hadn't really thought of as a strength, but they say it really is as it helps them to stay calm.

My weaknesses that matter (and what I plan to do about them)

Sometimes I can put off doing things I don't want to do but that are important. This sometimes matters a lot at work. When I find myself doing this I am going to bring to mind my 'do the right thing' strength. If the thing that I am putting off is really important I will use my desire to do the right thing to make me crack on and get it done!

I am not particularly good at data analysis. I often struggle on with it, sometimes working late. But I realize my deputy is really good at this and is always is keen to help and support me so I will talk to her about taking on this aspect of the job.

My overdone strengths

I love developing people and have had a couple of instances where I have stuck with people and tried to develop the undevelopable. Now that I know about strengths I realize my efforts with these particular people were never going to pay off. Again, using my 'do the right thing' strength will help me to avoid this situation.

My strengths map

My clear strengths	My previously hidden (or unknown) strengths
I love to be in charge	I am a calm person
I keep going when things are tough	
I love developing others	
It's important to me to do the right thing	
I have a strong work ethic	
Strengths I sometimes overdo	**Weaknesses**
Trying to develop others in areas where it's unrealistic	Data analysis
	Putting things off at times

MY STRENGTHS PROFILE

Me:

My Strengths Profile:

My best self: themes

My top strengths

-

  _____

  _____

-

  _____

  _____

-

  _____

  _____

-

  _____

  _____

-

  _____

  _____

Feedback from others

My weaknesses that matter (and what I plan to do about them)

My overdone strengths

My strengths map

My clear strengths	My previously hidden (or unknown) strengths
Strengths I sometimes overdo	**Weaknesses**

REFERENCES

PART ONE

[1] Mann, Annamarie and Harter, Jim. *The Worldwide Employee Engagement Crisis*, Gallup Business Journal (January 2016) http://www.gallup.com/businessjournal/188033/worldwide-employee-engagement-crisis.aspx?g_source=Business+Journal&g_medium=CardRelatedItems&g_campaign=tiles

[2] London Business School and Finance (LSBF) http://www.telegraph.co.uk/finance/jobs/11871751/Its-official-most-people-are-miserable-at-work.html

[3] Buckingham, Marcus. *Go Put Your Strengths to Work*, (Simon and Shuster 2007, New York), pg. 64

[4] David, Susan, *Positive Thinking Won't Make You Happy*, Washington Post (2016) https://www.washingtonpost.com/news/inspired-life/wp/2016/09/23/forcing-positive-thinking-wont-make-you-happy-says-this-harvard-psychologist/?utm_term=.f498373ca141

[5] Cuddy, Amy. *Your Body Language Shapes Who You Are*, TED Global (2012) https://www.ted.com/talks/amy_cuddy_your_body_language_shapes_who_you_are

PART THREE

[6] Rigoni, Brandon and Nelson, Bailey. *Retaining Employees: How Much Does Money Matter?* Gallup (January 2016) http://www.gallup.com/businessjournal/188399/retaining-employees-money-matter.aspx

[7] Sorenson, Susan. *How Employees' Strengths Make Your Company Stronger,* Gallup Business Journal (February 2014) http://www.gallup.com/businessjournal/167462/employees-strengths-company-stronger.aspx

[8] Newman, Kira M. *Happy Couples Focus on Each Other's Strengths,* Greater Good Magazine (May 2017) https://greatergood.berkeley.edu/article/item/happy_couples_focus_on_each_others_strengths

PART FIVE

[9] Deayton, A and Kahneman, D, *High Income Improves Evaluation of Life But Not Emotional Well-being*, Centre for Health and Wellbeing, Princeton University (July 2010). https://www.princeton.edu/~deaton/downloads/deaton_kahneman_high_income_improves_evaluation_August2010.pdf

[10] Baumeister, Roy F, Vohs, Kathleen D, Aaker, Jennifer and Garbinsky, Emily N. *Some Key Differences Between a Happy Life and a Meaningful Life*, Journal of Positive Psychology, Vol. 8, Issue 6, Pages 505-516 (2013)

FURTHER READING

Anderson, Simone, *The Networking Book* (LID 2015)

Bibb, Sally, *Strengths-Based Recruitment and Development: A Practical Guide to Transforming Talent Management Strategy for Business Results* (Kogan Page 2016)

Boniwell, Ilona, *Positive Psychology in a Nutshell* (Personal Wellbeing Centre 2006)

Buckingham, Marcus, *Go Put Your Strengths to Work* (Simon and Schuster 20007)

Csikszentmihalyi, Mihaly, *Flow: The Classic Work on How to Achieve Happiness* (Random House 2002)

Gratton, Lynda and Scott, Andrew, *The 100 Year Life* (Bloomsbury London 2016)

Hawkins, Peter, *No Regrets on Sunday* (Vermilion 2012)

Munz-Jones, Neil, *The Reluctant Networker* (HotHive Books 2010)

Parkin, John C, *F**k It – Do What You Love* (Hay House UK Limited 2016)

ACKNOWLEDGEMENTS

I've always thought that it was easier to write long pieces than short ones. This little book was proof of that. It has been deceptively challenging to write. Many people helped and encouraged me in this endeavour. My thanks and gratitude go to:

My family, friends, colleagues and clients for your enthusiasm and support of The Strengths Revolution and this book.

Mary Nathan for your early feedback and suggestions on the structure.

Sally Blake, Carmel Cahill, Jo Dale, Kate Monro, Ceris Morris, David North, Kate Saunders, Elly Smith and Millie Townsend for your thoughtful review of the draft plan and manuscript.

Martin Liu for commissioning the book and Sara Taheri, Liz Cooley, Niki Mullin and the wonderful team at LID for making it happen.

Charlie Haynes at Urban Writers' Retreat for providing such a lovely space to write.

All the people I've worked with and mentored – because of you I knew what was needed in this book.

ABOUT THE AUTHOR

SALLY BIBB is a leading figure in The Strengths Revolution and founder of Engaging Minds, a strengths consultancy that has achieved outstanding results for many well-known organizations including the NHS, Olympics, Saga and Starbucks.

She is an award winning author of several business books including *Strengths-based-Recruitment and Development*.

Sally has worked all over the world. Before founding Engaging Minds she worked at The Economist Group and in the telecommunications sector.

She has a BA (Hons) in Social Sciences, an MSc in Change Agent Skills and Strategies from the University of Surrey and is a Fellow of the Royal Society of Arts.

Her mission is to spread the strengths message beyond the organizational world to help people of all ages and life stages.